Staffordshire Library and Information Services

Staffordshire
County Council

{ Seasons }

by Janet Allison Brown

{ Contents }

THIS EDITION:
© 2015 Book Life
King's Lynn
Norfolk PE30 4HG

FIRST EDITION:
2003 © Aladdin Books Ltd
PO Box 53987
London SW15 2SF

ISBN: 978-1-910512-33-3
All rights reserved.
Printed in Malaysia

A CIP record for this
book is available from
the British Library.

LITERACY CONSULTANT
Ann Hawken, Oxford Brookes University
Westminster Institute of Education

DESIGNED BY
Ian McMullen

EDITED BY
Grace Jones

Have you ever felt the hot sun in summer or icy winds in winter?

Have you seen blossom in spring or the falling leaves in autumn?

These are the seasons, the different times of the year.

{ **Boats in summer** }

Each season brings changes. Days grow longer in spring, then grow shorter again in autumn.

In summer the sun shines longest – it is a good time for a boat ride!

Every year, the weather changes from warm to hot to cool to cold.

In lots of countries, the coldest days of the year are in winter. Rain turns to snow and people stay indoors.

{ Spring }

{ Apple blossom }

How can you tell when it is spring?
Little buds appear on the trees.

In a few weeks, these turn into little
flowers, called blossom.

Spring rain

Spring is when things start to grow.
It is often cold and wet.

After a while the days grow longer
and the skies are brighter. But the
rains keeps falling!

{ Splashing in puddles }

Spring can be a time for umbrellas and splashing in puddles!

{ Ploughing }

{ Seeds grow }

In spring, farmers plough their fields and plant seeds in the ground.

The spring rain falls on the seeds and helps them to grow.

{ Chicks }

Many baby animals are born now.
Birds build nests and lay their eggs.

In a few weeks the eggs hatch
into chicks.

{ **Summer flowers** }

{ Little apples }

Summer is full of bright colours.

The trees are heavy with leaves and some fields are a blanket of flowers.

{ At the
beach }

{ In the country }

Summer is the season for being outdoors. The days are long and bright.

The hot, sunny weather is perfect for long walks in the country or days at the beach.

{Butterfly}

{Bee}

In summer, the grass grows tall and thick.

Butterflies flutter from flower to flower.

{ Rabbit }

Bees buzz through the air. They are busy using flowers to make honey.

You will often see rabbits nibble on grass. Be quiet or their long ears will hear you coming.

{ Autumn leaves }

{ Ripe apples }

In autumn, the weather becomes cooler and the days grow shorter.

The leaves change from green to gold and red. They fall from the trees and blow about in the autumn wind.

In autumn, farmers are busy picking fruit and other crops.

This farmer grows grapes. When they are dry, they will be called raisins. Do you like eating raisins?

{ Squirrel }

{ Blackbird }

Animals know that in autumn cold weather is on its way.

Squirrels gather nuts to eat in winter. Birds feed on berries, and some fly away to warmer places.

{ Winter trees }

{ Bare branches }

In winter the weather is cold.
The days are short and dark.

Most trees are bare and brown. They
make strange shapes against the sky

{ Icicles }

When it gets really cold, snow falls and the world turns white.

Drops of water become icicles.

{ Hare }

{ Mouse }

This mouse sleeps through the winter.
Some hares grow a white coat to hide
in the snow.

Under the snow, nothing grows
– everything waits for spring!

{ Rainforest }

In some places the seasons are all alike.

Rainforests are always hot, but some seasons are more rainy.

{ Desert }

{ South Pole }

When it does not rain, deserts have no seasons.

The South Pole has two seasons. The sun shines almost all the time in summer, and almost never in winter.

Can you work out what season it is by looking at animals or plants?

Look at these pictures and see!

Clue: Look at pages 7, 11, 16, 19, 24 and 25.

{ Answers on page 32 }

1

2

Look at these four pictures of the same tree.

Do you know which one shows it in spring, summer, autumn or winter?

3

{ Answers on page 32 }

4

{ Index }

{ Answers to questions }

Pages 28-29 – Blossom appears in spring • This hare has a white coat in winter • You see most butterflies in summer • Apples are ripe in aumtumn • Most chicks hatch from eggs in spring • Icicles appear on cold days • Pages 30-31 – 1 shows the tree in spring • 2 shows the tree in autumn • 3 shows the tree in winter • 4 shows the tree in summer.

{ Photocredits }

Abbreviations: l-left, r-right, b-bottom, t-top, c-centre, m-middle
All images are courtesy of Shutterstock.com
Cover — Elena Zajchikova. Page 1,8 — Kichigin. 3 ,12— LilKar. 5 — Oxa. 6 — Hitdelight. 7 — Liga Alksne. 9 — Dasha Petrenko. 9inset — Brian A Jackson. 10 — Elena Elisseeva. 10inset — Bogdan Wankowicz. 11 — PCHT. 13 — Zaharia Bogdan Rares. 14 — altanaka. 15 — Monkey Business Images. 16t — artjazz. 16b — Valentina Proskurina. 17 — Subbotina Anna. 18 — Konstantin Sutyagin. 19 — Jorge Salcedo. 20 — mythja. 21t — Neil Burton. 21b — Gertjan Hooijer. 22-23 — balounm. 24 — Kuttelvaserova Stuchelova. 25l — Peter Wey. 25r — BMJ. 26 — Egon Zitter. 27t — Marques. 27b — Chaikovskiy Igor. 30-31 — Smit.